United States Government Accountability Office

GAO

Report to the Ranking Member, Subcommittee on Technology, Information Policy, Intergovernmental Relations and Procurement Reform, Committee on Oversight and Government Reform, House of Representatives

June 2012

THRIFT SAVINGS PLAN

‖‖‖‖‖‖‖‖‖‖‖‖‖‖‖‖‖

I0425843

Adding a Socially Responsible Index Fund Presents Challenges

GAO

Accountability ★ Integrity ★ Reliability

GAO-12-664

GAO
Accountability * Integrity * Reliability

Highlights

Highlights of GAO-12-664, a report to Ranking Member, Subcommittee on Technology, Information Policy, Intergovernmental Relations and Procurement Reform Committee on Oversight and Government Reform, House of Representatives

June 2012

THRIFT SAVINGS PLAN

Adding a Socially Responsible Index Fund Presents Challenges

Why GAO Did This Study

Socially responsible investment— investment made on the basis of environmental, social, religious, or corporate governance criteria— in U.S.-based mutual funds exceeded $300 billion in value in 2010. TSP—a $308 billion retirement plan with more than 4.5 million participants—currently offers five distinct low-cost investment options, and is authorized to offer a service that enables direct participant investment in mutual funds outside TSP. GAO was asked to consider the value of adding an SRI option to TSP. GAO examined: (1) What challenges might TSP face in adopting an SRI option? (2) How would the addition of an index fund tracking an SRI index have affected past TSP stock portfolio performance? (3) How do the performance and costs of SRI mutual funds compare to those of non-SRI mutual funds?

To analyze the challenges surrounding SRI, GAO interviewed federal officials, SRI experts, and representatives of public retirement plans that had considered SRI adoption. To examine the impact of adding an SRI fund to the existing TSP funds, GAO analyzed monthly benchmark return data. To examine mutual fund performance trends and costs, GAO analyzed historical summary data on US-based mutual funds.

GAO provided a copy of this draft report to the Board, the Department of Labor, and the Department of the Treasury for review and comment. None of the agencies provided formal comments on the report.

What GAO Recommends

This report contains no recommendations.

View GAO-12-664. For more information, contact Charles Jeszeck at (202) 512-7215 or jeszeckc@gao.gov.

What GAO Found

Officials at the Thrift Savings Plan (TSP) and the other public retirement plans that had considered socially responsible investment (SRI) associated a number of common challenges with SRI adoption. While none of these plans were identical to TSP in scope or demographics, many plan officials shared similar challenges and concerns with TSP. For example, they identified participant demand, SRI screening criteria, and costs as the most common challenges. Officials at public retirement plans that had adopted SRI cited some short-term benefits of SRI, such as providing participants an opportunity to invest in accordance with their values, but said that the long-term benefits were unknown.

When compared to the past performance of the TSP stock portfolio, the addition of a hypothetical SRI index fund tracking the best-performing U.S.-based SRI stock index would not have both increased returns and lowered volatility in any allocation scenario that GAO tested. Specifically, over the last 20 years, if TSP had included such an SRI index fund in its existing stock portfolio, it could have resulted in (1) lower returns and lower volatility, (2) lower returns and higher volatility, or (3) higher returns and higher volatility, based on GAO's analysis of evenly distributed portfolio allocations. The managers of the SRI index explained the difference in the index's performance over the last 20 years was a result of having different sector weightings than the overall market to align with the fund's SRI strategy. Moreover, the addition of this SRI fund would have resulted in overlap with the TSP stock portfolio, and would not have provided a substantial opportunity for additional portfolio diversification.

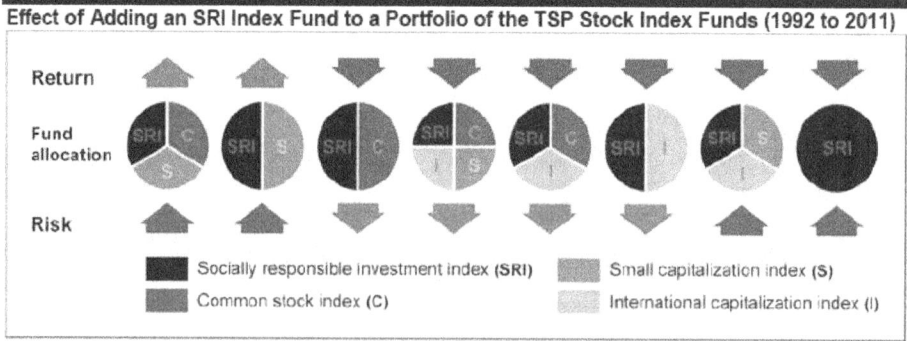

Effect of Adding an SRI Index Fund to a Portfolio of the TSP Stock Index Funds (1992 to 2011)

Source: GAO analysis of annual rates of total return based on monthly total return data from Morningstar Inc.

Looking more broadly at SRI mutual funds—the most common form of SRI in the United States—GAO found the comparative performance of SRI and non-SRI mutual funds to vary by asset class while costs were nearly the same. Regarding performance, SRI bond mutual funds had better risk-adjusted performance than their non-SRI counterparts over the last 15 years, while SRI stock and balanced funds did not. However, after controlling for various factors such as fund size, SRI stock mutual funds had better estimated performance as well. Regarding costs, in fiscal year 2010, the costs of SRI institutional grade mutual funds were similar to their non-SRI counterparts. Although TSP participants cannot currently invest in mutual funds through TSP, the Federal Retirement Thrift Investment Board (Board) is authorized to offer a mutual fund window if it determines that it is in the best interests of participants.

_____ **United States Government Accountability Office**

Contents

Figures

Abbreviations

Board	Federal Retirement Thrift Investment Board
C Fund	Common Stock Index Investment Fund
DB	defined benefit
DC	defined contribution
ESG	environmental, social, and corporate governance
ERISA	Employee Retirement Income Security Act of 1974
ETAC	Employee Thrift Advisory Council
FERS	Federal Employees' Retirement System
FERSA	Federal Employees' Retirement System Act of 1986
F Fund	Fixed Income Investment Fund
G Fund	Government Securities Investment Fund
I Fund	International Stock Index Investment Fund
S Fund	Small Capitalization Stock Index Investment Fund
SRI	socially responsible investment
TSP	Thrift Savings Plan

June 26, 2012

The Honorable Gerald E. Connolly
Ranking Member
Subcommittee on Technology,
    Information Policy,
    Intergovernmental Relations
    and Procurement Reform
Committee on Oversight
    and Government Reform
House of Representatives

Dear Mr. Connolly:

Since its inception in 1986, the federal government's Thrift Savings Plan (TSP) has become a central component of federal employees' retirement savings. Intended to resemble 401(k) pension plans in the private sector, TSP allows employees to contribute a portion of their current compensation through payroll salary deductions and to allocate their contributions and any associated earnings among the available investment options. As of February 2012, TSP held about $308 billion in retirement assets and had more than 4.5 million participants, making it one of the largest retirement savings plans in the United States.

The Federal Employees' Retirement System Act of 1986 (FERSA) established TSP and the Federal Retirement Thrift Investment Board (Board), an independent agency in the executive branch, to administer it.[1] The five-member, presidentially appointed Board must manage TSP prudently and solely in the interest of the participants and their beneficiaries and cannot exercise the voting rights associated with ownership of securities in TSP. FERSA also established three TSP investment funds: the Government Securities Investment Fund (G Fund), Common Stock Index Investment Fund (C Fund), and Fixed Income Investment Fund (F Fund). In 1996, Congress authorized TSP to broaden its offerings with the International Stock Index Investment Fund (I Fund)

---

[1] 5 U.S.C. § 8472.

and Small Capitalization Stock Index Investment Fund (S Fund). Since August 2005, TSP participants also have had the option to choose one of five lifecycle funds, which diversify participant accounts among the G, F, C, S, and I Funds using investment mixes tailored for different retirement time horizons.

Congress has proposed legislation to require TSP to offer additional investment options in an effort to give participants and beneficiaries greater investment choice. Several of these proposals have sought to require TSP to include a responsible investment index fund that would track a market index comprised of stocks that were prescreened for corporate governance, environmental practices, workplace relations and benefits, product safety and impact, international operations and human rights, involvement with repressive regimes, and community relations.[2] Commonly referred to as socially responsible investment (SRI), this kind of investment strategy seeks to generate long-term competitive financial returns while realizing positive societal impact by investing in accordance with one's values or certain environmental, social, or corporate governance criteria. Investment in SRI mutual funds—the most common SRI vehicle—exceeded $300 billion in 2010. Congress asked us to examine the value of adding an additional investment option to TSP in the form of an SRI index fund. In response to this request, we examined the following questions:

- What challenges might TSP face in adopting an SRI option?

- How would the addition of an index fund tracking an SRI index have affected past TSP stock fund portfolio performance?

- How do the performance and costs of SRI mutual funds compare to non-SRI mutual funds?

To determine the challenges associated with SRI, we reviewed relevant federal laws and regulations related to FERSA and TSP, and literature. We also interviewed officials from TSP, the Employee Thrift Advisory Council (ETAC), investment management or consultant firms, and a

---

[2]The Financial Industry Regulatory Authority defines index funds as passive funds that seek to replicate the performance of a market index instead of outperforming it. Index funds differ from mutual funds which are investment companies that pool money from many investors and invest it based on specific investment goals.

nonrepresentative sample of 15 public pension plans. To identify our sample, we contacted plans that were signatories of the United Nations' *Principles for Responsible Investment* and employed a snowball sampling technique based on recommendations of interviewees. To assess how the addition of an index fund tracking an SRI index would have affected past TSP stock fund portfolio performance, we identified the best performing U.S.-based SRI stock index based on 10-year risk-adjusted performance data, and analyzed its potential impact on the TSP stock portfolio over the past 20 years (1992 through 2011).[3] Because this analysis is strictly based on past performance, this result does not guarantee or imply that the addition of an SRI index would have the same effect on future TSP stock fund portfolio performance. To determine how the performance and costs of SRI mutual funds compared with those of non-SRI mutual funds, we analyzed historical performance data for several time periods over the past 15 years (dating back from December 2011)—the longest time period for which data were available—and cost data from fiscal year 2010. We focused our analysis exclusively on three share classes of mutual funds—institutional, front-load, and no-load—of U.S. domiciled open-end mutual funds, which experts identified as the most common form of SRI funds.[4] To better demonstrate the full range of performance and costs trends between SRI and non-SRI mutual funds, we analyzed funds by subcategories such as share class, and also ran regressions to control for factors such as fund asset size and investment strategy.

We assessed the reliability of the quantitative data used in this engagement by reviewing related documentation, interviewing knowledgeable officials, reviewing related internal controls, comparing to published data, and tracing a selection of data to source documentation. Based on this evaluation, we determined these data were reliable for the purposes of this report. Additional details regarding our methodology can be found in appendix I.

---

[3]We selected the best performing SRI stock index from the five U.S.-based SRI stock indices with at least a 10-year history that were active as of December 2011. (We identified three other U.S.-based SRI stock indices that did not have a 10-year history.) We did not run a similar analysis on an SRI bond index because no U.S-based SRI bond indices exist.

[4]Morningstar, Inc., identified three share classes of mutual funds—institutional, front-load, and no-load—as the most common share classes used by institutional investors. We refer to these three share classes together as institutional grade mutual funds.

We conducted this performance audit from July 2011 to June 2012 in accordance with generally accepted government auditing standards. Those standards require that we plan and perform the audit to obtain sufficient, appropriate evidence to provide a reasonable basis for our findings and conclusions based on our audit objectives. We believe that the evidence obtained provides a reasonable basis for our findings and conclusions based on our audit objectives.

Background

The Thrift Savings Plan

FERSA created TSP to provide options for retirement planning and encourage personal retirement saving among the federal workforce. Most federal workers are allowed to participate in TSP, which is available to federal and postal employees, including members of Congress and congressional employees and members of the uniformed services, and members of the judicial branch. TSP is structured to allow eligible federal employees to contribute a fixed percentage of their annual base pay or a flat amount, subject to Internal Revenue Service limits, into an individual tax-deferred account. Additionally, Federal Employees' Retirement System (FERS) participants are eligible for automatic 1-percent contributions and limited matching contributions from the employing federal agency. TSP provides federal (and in most cases, state) income tax deferral on contributions and their related earnings, similar to those offered by many private sector 401(k)-type pension plans.[5] As is typical in defined contribution (DC) plans, TSP allows participants to manage their accounts and conduct a variety of transactions similar to those available to 401(k) participants, including reallocating contributions or account

---

[5]FERSA created FERS. As part of FERS, TSP is also part of the current three-part retirement system for federal employees, which includes Social Security benefits, the basic defined benefit (DB) plan, and TSP. The Office of Personnel Management trains retirement counselors about each part of the plan. Prior to FERS, most federal employees were covered by the Civil Service Retirement System.

balances, borrowing from the account, making withdrawals, or purchasing annuities.[6]

Administration of TSP falls under the purview of the Board, an agency established by Congress under FERSA. The Board is composed of five members appointed by the President, with the advice and consent of the Senate. They are authorized to appoint the executive director who hires additional personnel, and ETAC—a 15-member council that provides advice to the Board and the executive director on the investment policies and administration of TSP.[7] The Board is responsible for establishing policies for the investment and management of TSP, as well as administration of the plan. The executive director and Board staff are responsible for implementing the Board's policies and managing the day-to-day operations of TSP, prescribing regulations to administer FERSA, and other duties. The Board members and the executive director serve as plan fiduciaries.[8] FERSA has other investment policy provisions, such as who can exercise voting rights associated with the ownership of stocks held by TSP.[9] For example, the Board and the executive director may not exercise voting rights associated with the ownership of TSP securities.

The Board has less discretion than private sector plan sponsors in setting investment policy because the investment options available to TSP participants are outlined in federal law, whereas private sector plan

---

[6]Pension plans may be classified either as DB or as DC plans. DB plans promise to provide, generally, a fixed level of monthly retirement income for life that is typically determined by a formula based on particular factors specified by the plan, such as salary, years of service, or age at retirement regardless of how the plan's investments perform. In contrast, benefits from DC plans will vary with the contributions to and the performance of the investments in individual accounts, which may fluctuate in value.

[7]5 U.S.C. § 8473.

[8]Similar to fiduciaries in private pension plan under the Employee Retirement Income Security Act of 1974 (ERISA), TSP fiduciaries are the persons who have discretionary control or authority over the management or administration of the plan, including management of the plan's assets. TSP fiduciaries are required to perform their responsibilities in the interest of participants and beneficiaries for the exclusive purpose of providing benefits to participants and their beneficiaries and defraying the reasonable expenses of administering the TSP. Other fiduciary responsibilities include the duty to act prudently and, to the extent permitted by law, to diversify the investment of the fund so as to minimize the risk of large losses, unless under the circumstances it is clearly prudent not to do so.

[9]5 U.S.C. § 8438(f).

sponsors have greater discretion in choosing which investment options to offer participants.[10] In addition, Congress must amend FERSA to approve a change in TSP investment options offered to participants. TSP's authorizing statute specifies the number and types of funds available to participants, and requires that some of these funds track indexes, which are broad, diversified market indicators. The Board may select the particular indices for the funds to follow as well as review the investment options and suggest additional funds. The Board has developed investment policies for each TSP fund. These policies, which the Board reaffirms quarterly, provide the rationale for selecting the fund's investments. Table 1 shows FERSA requirements and Board policies regarding each fund and its underlying index.

Table 1: Investment Requirements for Existing TSP Funds

Fund	FERSA investment requirements	Board investment policies
G Fund	Treasury securities specially issued to TSP with a maturity determined by the executive director that provide the generally higher interest rates of securities with a term of at least 4 years [5 U.S.C. § 8438(a)(4)].	Short-term securities that mature in 1 to 4 days
F Fund	Fixed-income securities [5 U.S.C. § 8438(a)(3)].	An index including bonds and asset-backed securities to track the Barclay's Capital U.S. Aggregate Bond Index.
C Fund	A portfolio that tracks a broad index representing the U.S. stock market [5 U.S.C. § 8438(a)(1)].	An index of stocks of large to medium-sized companies to track the Standard & Poor's 500 Index.
S Fund	A portfolio that tracks a broad index representing U.S. stocks not included in the C Fund [5 U.S.C. § 8438(a)(3)(B)].	An index of stocks in small and medium-sized companies not represented in the Standard & Poor's 500 Index to track the Dow Jones Total Stock Market Completion Index.
I Fund	A portfolio that tracks a broad index representing international stock markets outside of the United States [5 U.S.C. § 8438(a)(5)].	An index of the stock markets of the developed world outside of the United States and Canada to track the Morgan Stanley Capital International Europe, Australasia, and Far East Index.

Source: GAO analysis of FERSA.

Members of Congress have introduced bills calling for new investment options to be added to TSP. In the past four sessions of Congress, a number of bills have been proposed to add investment options to TSP, including a corporate responsibility stock index fund, a precious metals investment fund, a real estate stock index fund, and a terror-free international investment option. In addition, Congress passed the Federal Retirement Reform Act of 2009, which among other things, authorized

---

[10]GAO, *Federal Retirement Thrift Investment Board: Many Responsibilities and Investment Policies Set by Congress*, GAO-07-611 (Washington, D.C.: June 21, 2007).

TSP to offer a service that would enable participants to invest in mutual funds outside TSP, if the Board determined that such a mutual fund window was in the best interests of participants.[11] The law stipulated that the Board had to ensure that any expenses charged for use of the mutual fund window would be borne solely by the participants who used it. The Board has not implemented the mutual fund window. According to TSP officials, both the Board and ETAC were similarly split on whether to include a mutual fund window and the Board tabled the discussion of the mutual fund window to address more immediate issues, such as adding a Roth TSP option.[12] They also noted that while TSP has not moved forward with adding a mutual fund window, it may at some future point.[13]

FERSA also requires the Board to defray reasonable expenses of administering TSP.[14] TSP's administrative expenses include management fees for each investment fund; the costs of operating and maintaining TSP's recordkeeping system; the cost of providing participant services; and the printing and mailing of notices, statements, and publications.[15] These expenses are offset by (1) forfeitures of agency automatic (1 percent) contributions made to employees who participated in the FERS

---

[11]Pub.L.No. 111-31, Div.B, §104, 123 Stat.1852, 1854 (codified at 5 U.S.C.§ 8438(b)(1)).

[12]The Roth TSP, as authorized by the Thrift Savings Plan Enhancement Act of 2009 (enacted June 22, 2009), allows federal civilian employees and members of the uniformed services to contribute after-tax dollars into the TSP for the first time. Both the contributions and their earnings will be tax-free when withdrawn, as long as IRS requirements are met. The Roth TSP option has been available to participants since May 2012.

[13]TSP's 2008 participant survey found that 39 percent of respondents said TSP would be a better program if it provided a self-directed mutual fund window, 24 percent said they would transfer some of their TSP account balance, and 10 percent would be willing to pay $100 annual fee to use the window. In a 2009 memorandum to the Board, the TSP executive director recommended the addition of a mutual fund window as an appealing feature to participants who sought more specialized or sophisticated TSP investments. Moreover, the window would allow participants to invest in funds that better matched their individualized risk tolerance or particular interests, such as SRI funds. According to the Department of Labor, the Board would need to consider the application of FERSA's fiduciary standards to the design and operation of such a mutual fund window.

[14]5 U.S.C. § 8477(b)(1)(A)(ii).

[15]According to the Department of Labor, the ERISA fiduciary standards governing investment decisions apply to an ERISA fiduciary's selection of a "socially responsible" mutual fund as a designated investment alternative under a private-sector pension plan.

but left federal service before becoming vested,[16] (2) other forfeitures, and (3) loan fees. Because these amounts are not sufficient to cover all of TSP's expenses, TSP participants share in the remainder of the costs. The cost to participants to invest in TSP is measured as an expense ratio of the total administrative expenses charged to a fund during a specific time period, divided by that fund's average balance for that specific time period. In 2011, expenses charged to each TSP account were approximately 25 cents per each $1,000 of investment, or 2.5 basis points. TSP's expense ratio typically falls below the average expense ratio of other 401(k) type plans.

Socially Responsible Investment

SRI—investment made on the basis of environmental, social, and corporate governance (ESG) criteria—is a global phenomenon and is growing in popularity in the United States. In 2006, the United Nations issued *Principles for Responsible Investment* that maintained a belief that ESG issues can affect the performance of investment portfolios and therefore must be given appropriate consideration by investors if they are to fulfill their fiduciary duty.[17] By supporting the principles, institutional investors commit to better align investors with broader societal goals while acting in the best long-term interests of their beneficiaries. Specifically, signatories agreed to

- incorporate ESG issues into investment analysis and decision-making processes,

- be active owners and incorporate ESG issues into their ownership policies and practices,

- seek appropriate disclosure on ESG issues by the entities in which they invest,

- promote acceptance and implementation of these principles within the investment industry to affect the performance of investment,

---

[16]Vesting means that the TSP provides that an employee's right to a benefit is nonforfeitable upon the attainment of the required period of service under the law.

[17]For more information on these principles, see http://www.unpri.org, accessed May 24, 2012.

- work together to enhance the effectiveness of the principles, and

- report on their activities and progress in implementing the principles.

In 2012, there were more than 1,000 asset owners, investment managers, and professional service partners that had committed to these principles worldwide—136 of them in the United States, according to the United Nations' website.

According to a 2010 report by US SIF[18]—a leading SRI advocacy group—U.S.-based, open-end mutual funds comprise the largest share of funds that incorporate ESG factors in the United States with holdings of more than $300 billion. Other investment vehicles that incorporate ESG factors include exchange traded funds, variable annuity products, and alternative investment funds. As shown in figure 1, the number of SRI mutual funds open to investors has grown steadily since 1990.

Figure 1: Cumulative Growth in the Number of U.S. Open-end SRI Mutual Funds, 1952 through 2011

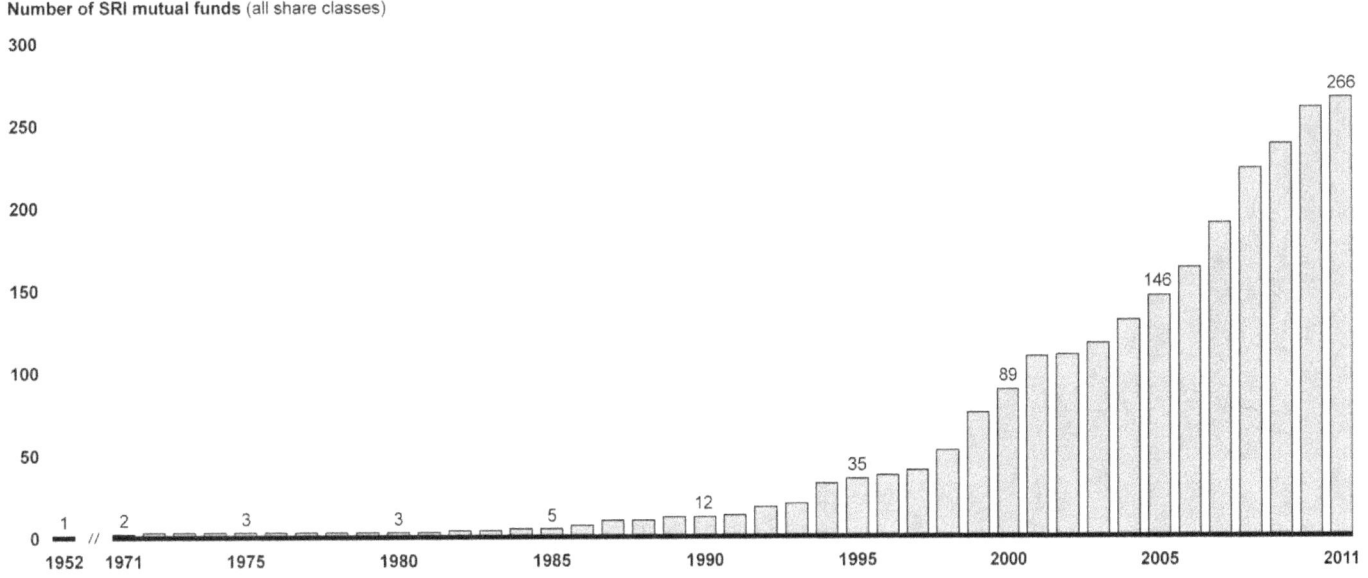

Source: GAO analysis of inception date data for SRI mutual funds active as of December 2011 from Morningstar, Inc. and US SIF

[18]US SIF was formerly known as the Social Investment Forum (SIF). US SIF is a U.S. membership association for professionals, firms, institutions, and organizations engaged in sustainable and responsible investing.

According to US SIF, there are three principal components of SRI:

- *Investment screening.* Investment screening is a practice of evaluating investment portfolios or mutual funds based on ESG criteria. Screening may involve including only strong performers, avoiding poor performers, or otherwise incorporating ESG factors into the process of investment analysis and management. Some responsible investors may avoid investment in companies whose products and business practices are harmful to individuals, communities, or the environment. Others may apply SRI screens to invest in companies that are leaders in adopting clean technologies and exceptional social and governance practices.

- *Shareholder advocacy.* Shareholder advocacy involves engaging companies directly on issues of concern through shareholder resolutions or proxy voting. Shareholder advocacy frequently involves the filing of shareholder resolutions to improve business practices. The resolutions are then voted on by all owners of a corporation. For example, shareholders can use resolutions to urge a company to improve its sustainability practices, such as by reducing its carbon emissions, or by improving its supply chain to ensure that labor laws are fully enforced. Similarly, proxy voting is the primary means by which shareholders are able to direct company management to act in a socially responsible manner. As partial owners of companies, shareholders have the right to weigh in on important issues through the process of proxy voting.

- *Community investing.* Community investing directs capital from investors and lenders to communities that are underserved by traditional financial services institutions. Community investing provides access to credit, equity, capital, and basic banking products that these communities would otherwise lack.

According to experts, investors pursue SRI for a variety of reasons. Some investors may invest solely in accordance with their values without considering financial implications. Other investors may pursue SRI for purely financial motives and seek out well managed companies that take steps to manage their ESG risks in the belief that these companies will outperform their competitors in the long run. SRI mutual funds offer a broad range of investment screens, including negative screens, which exclude industry sectors associated with certain products or processes; restricted screens, which set a threshold for investment in companies associated with certain products or processes; and positive screens, which include industry sectors associated with certain products, processes, or values, or invest in "best-in-class" companies that demonstrate the strongest record of incorporating ESG criteria into their business models. Figure 2 provides an overview of investment screens applied by current SRI mutual funds in the United States.

Figure 2: Investment Screens Applied by SRI Mutual Funds

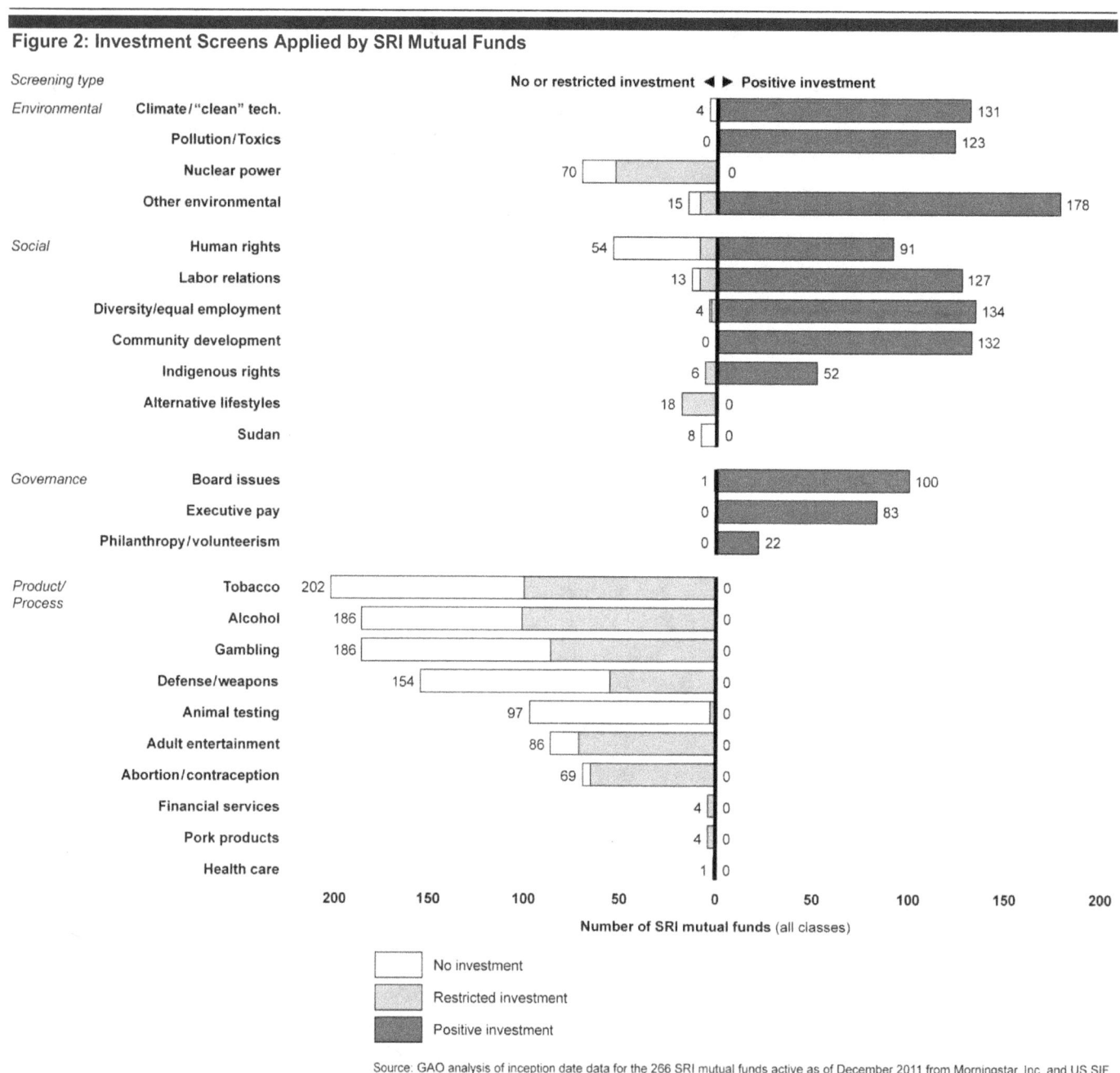

Source: GAO analysis of inception date data for the 266 SRI mutual funds active as of December 2011 from Morningstar, Inc. and US SIF.

Officials Identified Several Challenges to SRI Adoption and Said the Long-term Economic Benefits of SRI Were Unknown

Challenges

Officials at TSP and the other public retirement plans that had considered adding an SRI option associated a number of common challenges with the implementation of SRI. While none of the plan officials that we contacted had plans that were identical to TSP in terms of its federal scope or participant demographics, many of them shared similar challenges and concerns with TSP.[19] As shown in figure 3, participant demand, SRI screening criteria, and costs were the most common challenges identified by public retirement plans.

---

[19]We included responses from officials from three public DB plans who, like TSP officials, were responsible for managing plans with large asset holdings and large, diverse participant groups. Although the fiduciary role of these officials differed significantly from that of TSP officials in terms of their ability to pursue SRI, these officials identified other challenges that were similar to the challenges that TSP officials identified.

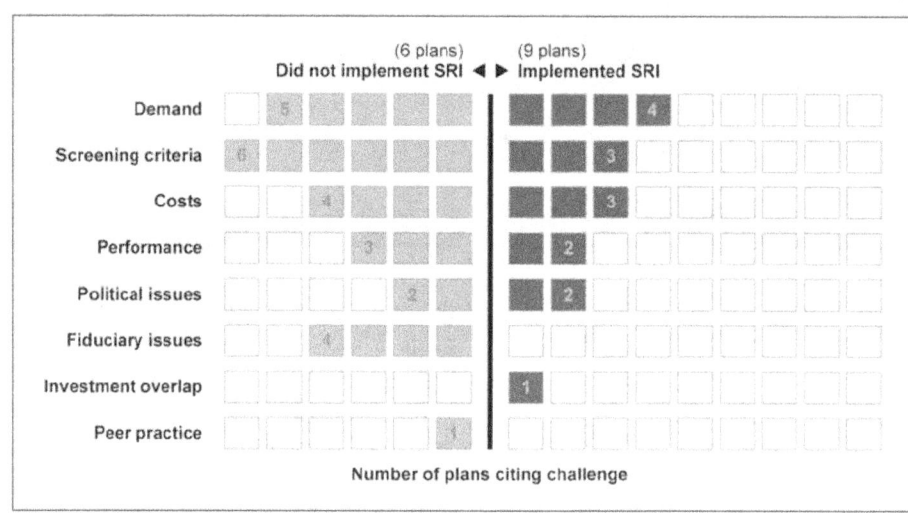

Figure 3: Number of Public Retirement Plans Identifying Challenges Associated with SRI Adoption Similar to Ones Identified by TSP Officials

Source: GAO analysis of interviews with public retirement plan officials

Participant Demand

TSP and most other public plan officials we contacted identified low participant demand for SRI as a challenge to adopting SRI. TSP officials told us that based on the results of their participant surveys and the experiences of ETAC there was little demand for an SRI fund among TSP participants. Specifically, they noted that the results of periodic participant surveys have consistently indicated that there was no overwhelming demand for any new investment options, including an SRI option.[20] In addition, ETAC members told us that they were unaware of demand for SRI among TSP participants. They said that they would respond if demand ever presented itself. While consultants and fund managers that we contacted reported a growing demand for SRI in the United States, public plan officials that we spoke with generally reported low participant interest in SRI adoption. Officials at several plans noted that continued pressure and repeated demands from small vocal groups of participants in support of SRI had been a principal driver in the plans' decision to have an SRI option. However, officials at several of these plans said that, while

---

[20]TSP's 2006-2007 participant survey found that none of the additional investment options that participants were asked to rate, including a socially responsible fund, had a majority of respondents who were willing to add the funds if there would be additional costs associated with utilizing those funds.

the SRI option did attract a small percentage of participants, overall participation in the SRI funds ranged from less than 0.5 percent (in one plan with 20 investment options) to about 10 percent (in a plan that offered 9 investment options).[21]

Selection of SRI criteria

TSP and most other public plan officials we contacted identified the difficulty of finding broadly acceptable SRI criteria as a distinct challenge to adopting SRI. According to TSP officials, different interpretations of what social criteria to apply to an SRI fund could lead to the need to develop multiple funds to satisfy participants. Officials also noted that it would be hard to reach agreement on what values an SRI fund should endorse. Moreover, officials at most of the other plans we contacted said that the lack of a common definition of SRI and the selection of SRI criteria was challenging. For example, officials at one plan noted that social issues were difficult to incorporate into an investment approach because, while some basic social issues, such as child labor, imprisonment, and forced slavery, were generally acceptable screens, reaching broad consensus on other issues, such as labor laws, workers' rights, weapons, guns, and tobacco, was more difficult. An official at another plan noted that it was incumbent upon participants to tell them what social policy they wished to pursue. Officials at the plans we contacted that considered selection of screening criteria to be a challenge overcame this challenge by either using an off-the shelf SRI fund, or relying on the expertise and experience of the SRI fund managers, or educating participants on why fund managers selected the investments they did.

Costs

TSP and other public plan officials we contacted had varied opinions on the degree to which the costs associated with the creation and administration of an SRI index fund presented a challenge to adopting SRI. According to TSP officials, the costs to create a new index fund would be considerable. In addition, they said an SRI index fund would cost more because it requires additional screening and monitoring. Under TSP's current cost structure, any costs associated with a new SRI index fund would be borne by all participants whether or not they chose to

---

[21]This range of participation rates in SRI funds is not a reflection on SRI as a viable investment option. For example, plans with more than 10 investment options could have 10 percent of participants investing in each option, including the SRI option. In contrast, plans like TSP with fewer investment options might consider a 10-percent SRI participation rate low when compared to the participation rates in the plan's other investment options.

GAO-12-664 Thrift Savings Plan

invest in the SRI index fund.[22] Other public plan officials we contacted had varied opinions on the degree to which these costs presented a challenge. While there would be certain upfront costs associated with adding an SRI fund, which could include member communication and manager selection, officials at several plans said that adding a new fund to its existing portfolio would not adversely affect administrative costs. According to some investment managers we contacted, the key factors affecting cost of any fund are (1) its asset size—the larger the asset base, the better the economies of scale and the lower the overall cost ratio—and (2) whether the fund's investment strategy requires active management or passively tracking of a market index.

Fiduciary Issues

While TSP and some public plan officials we contacted asserted that their role as fiduciary was a challenge in that it precluded the adoption of SRI, officials at other public plans with an SRI option said there were no fiduciary concerns surrounding the inclusion of an SRI option in a DC plan. According to a 1990 memorandum sent from the TSP executive director to the Board, Congress considered and rejected the concept of social investment when creating TSP. The memorandum noted that the strict fiduciary provisions of the law, which require the Board to discharge its responsibilities solely in the interest of participants, excluded the possibility of social investing, and that any authorization outside the realm of interest of all participants would be inconsistent with the notion of employee ownership of TSP assets. Officials at all of the public plans that had not implemented an SRI option considered fiduciary issues a challenge to adopting SRI, while officials at other plans did not. For example, an official at one plan with an SRI option stated that fiduciary duty was not a challenge when adding an SRI fund to the investment options to a DC plan because participants have individual account ownership, are free to choose how they invest, and must assume responsibility for any risks associated with the underlying investments. One plan official noted that the fiduciary responsibility of a DC plan extends to exercising due diligence in the selection of a fund manager, providing appropriate participant communications about the fund, offering enough investment options, and acting in the best interest of the majority of participants.

---

[22]According to TSP regulations, the amount of accrued administrative expenses not covered by forfeitures (agency contributions made to employees who leave federal service before vesting) and not directly attributable to an individual fund (such as fund management fees) are charged on a pro rata basis to all TSP funds, based on the respective fund balances on the last business day of the prior month end.

Concerns about Political Interference

TSP and some public plan officials that we contacted asserted that investment decisions made on any basis other than the economic welfare of participants could present a challenge in that it would expose the plan to potential political interference. In its 2006 investment option review, a consulting firm hired by TSP eliminated SRI from consideration in part on the grounds that identifying screening criteria that all could agree to would be difficult to find and likely draw attention from opposing parties of interest.[23] According to the 1990 memorandum from the TSP executive director, the laws that established the current TSP funds prevent the political manipulation of TSP funds, and officials told us that TSP has taken steps in the past to avoid political interference. Officials at the public plans we contacted had different views on the extent to which political interference was a challenge. For example, officials at some public plans that did not implement SRI identified political interference as one of the reasons they chose not to do so. On the other hand, officials at other public plans that had implemented SRI said that political interference was not a challenge. For example, officials at one public plan noted that the state's legislative mandate to maximize returns and improve levels of risk prevented political interference. An official at another public plan that adopted SRI told us that although they had anticipated political interference by state officials following their decision to divest from alcohol or tobacco companies, it had not materialized.

SRI Performance

Officials at TSP and some other public plans identified SRI fund performance as a challenge to adopting an SRI fund. According to TSP officials, participants who allocated assets to an SRI fund instead of a standard fund that included all relevant companies would narrow the number of companies in which they were indirectly investing, thereby limiting their exposure to the performance of the broader, more diversified market. While officials at some public plans that we contacted believed that SRI funds had lower performance than other funds, other officials had mixed views on whether the performance of SRI funds was any more challenging than the performance of non-SRI funds. Officials at several plans, which had considered but not implemented SRI, cited SRI performance as a reason for not incorporating SRI in their plans. Officials at one plan said they would reconsider offering an SRI fund if it demonstrated better long-term performance than non-SRI funds.

---

[23]See "Investment Option Review for the Federal Thrift Savings Plan," Ennis Knupp and Associates, Oct. 2006. The report is accessible on the Board's website: http://www.frtib.gov/FOIA/index.html, accessed June 15, 2012.

However, officials at several other plans that implemented SRI told us that the SRI fund produced comparable and sometimes better returns than other funds in their portfolio. Officials at one plan said the plan would terminate its working relationship with an external fund manager if its SRI investments did not perform as well as other funds.

Peer Practice

While TSP officials considered the lack of peer implementation of SRI as a challenge to adopting an SRI fund, officials at other public plans we contacted said that it was not a challenge. As part of its investment options review in 2006, a consulting firm advised TSP that SRI funds were not a common practice among TSP's peers and identified this criterion as a reason for eliminating SRI from further consideration. According to TSP officials, the fact that similar plans had not adopted SRI was a challenge in that TSP had no precedent to follow. We found a number plans similar in asset size and membership to TSP that applied SRI principles through investment screening. Officials at several plans we contacted said that peer implementation of SRI did not factor in their decision to incorporate SRI into their investment strategy.

Investment Overlap

Officials at most of the public plans we contacted had no restrictions regarding investment overlap between funds and thus did not view such overlap as a challenge to adopting SRI. According to TSP officials, the Board is permitted to suggest legislation to address any gaps in investment options as long as there is no evident overlap. In the past, for example, TSP proposed legislation authorizing the addition of the S Fund and the I Fund to provide participants with options for greater diversification of investments in the small capitalization and international markets. According to TSP officials, each of the current funds tracks different companies in different segments of the overall financial market without overlap, helping to reduce the risk of incurring large losses on a broader portfolio. Officials at other public plans, which did not face the same restrictions as TSP, said that overlap was not a consideration, and that certain amount of overlap with existing investments was both expected and accepted. Some officials noted that the purpose of SRI was to select companies that met certain criteria and provided an alternative investment choice.

Benefits

Officials at some of the nine public plans we contacted that offered an SRI option cited some short-term benefits associated with SRI but said that the long-term benefits were unknown. For example, officials at several plans noted that the greatest benefit of having an SRI option is giving participants broader investment choice and an opportunity to make a statement in the way they invest. Officials at other plans said that having an SRI option could serve as a recruiting tool for the plan in that it encouraged more eligible employees to join the plan. Regarding the long-term benefits of SRI, officials at two of the public plans stated that it was still too early to judge the benefit of SRI. As one plan official noted, responsible investment involves making investment decisions that are important to the long-term value and profitability of a company over time.

Adding an SRI Index Fund Would Not Have Improved Past TSP Portfolio Performance in Most Allocation Scenarios

When compared to the past performance of the TSP stock portfolio (the C, S, and I Funds), the addition of a hypothetical SRI index fund tracking the best-performing U.S.-based SRI stock index would not have both increased returns and lowered volatility in any allocation scenario we tested. Specifically, over the last 20 years, if TSP had included such an SRI index fund (SRI Fund) in its existing stock portfolio,[24] it could have resulted in (1) lower returns and lower volatility, (2) lower returns and higher volatility, or (3) higher returns and higher volatility, based on our analysis of evenly distributed portfolio allocations containing the SRI Fund against the TSP stock portfolio alone (a C, S, and I Funds combination).[25] For example, as shown in figure 4, adding the SRI Fund to the existing TSP stock funds (an SRI, C, S, and I Funds combination) would have resulted in lower returns and lower volatility; substituting the SRI Fund for the C Fund (an SRI, S, and I Funds combination) would have resulted in lower returns and higher volatility; and substituting the SRI Fund for the I Fund (an SRI, C, and S Funds combination) would have resulted in higher returns and higher volatility.[26] Because this analysis is strictly based on past performance, this result does not guarantee or imply that

---

[24]TSP's stock portfolio includes TSP's three stock index funds—C fund, S fund, and I fund. We did not include a similar analysis of bond funds because no U.S.-based SRI bond indices exist.

[25]For example, four-way combinations allocate 25 percent to each fund and three-way combinations allocate 33 percent to each fund. Portfolios were rebalanced annually to maintain even distributions. In this section, returns are measured by the compound rate of return and volatility is measured by standard deviation of annual returns. Standard deviation is a statistical measure of the range of a fund's performance. When a fund has a high standard deviation, its range of performance has been very wide, indicating that there is a greater potential for volatility.

[26]For more information on the annual compound rates of return and standard deviation of these funds, see appendix II.

the addition of an SRI index would have the same effect on future TSP stock fund portfolio performance.

Figure 4: Effect of Adding a Hypothetical TSP SRI Index Fund on Past TSP Stock Portfolio Performance, 1992 to 2011

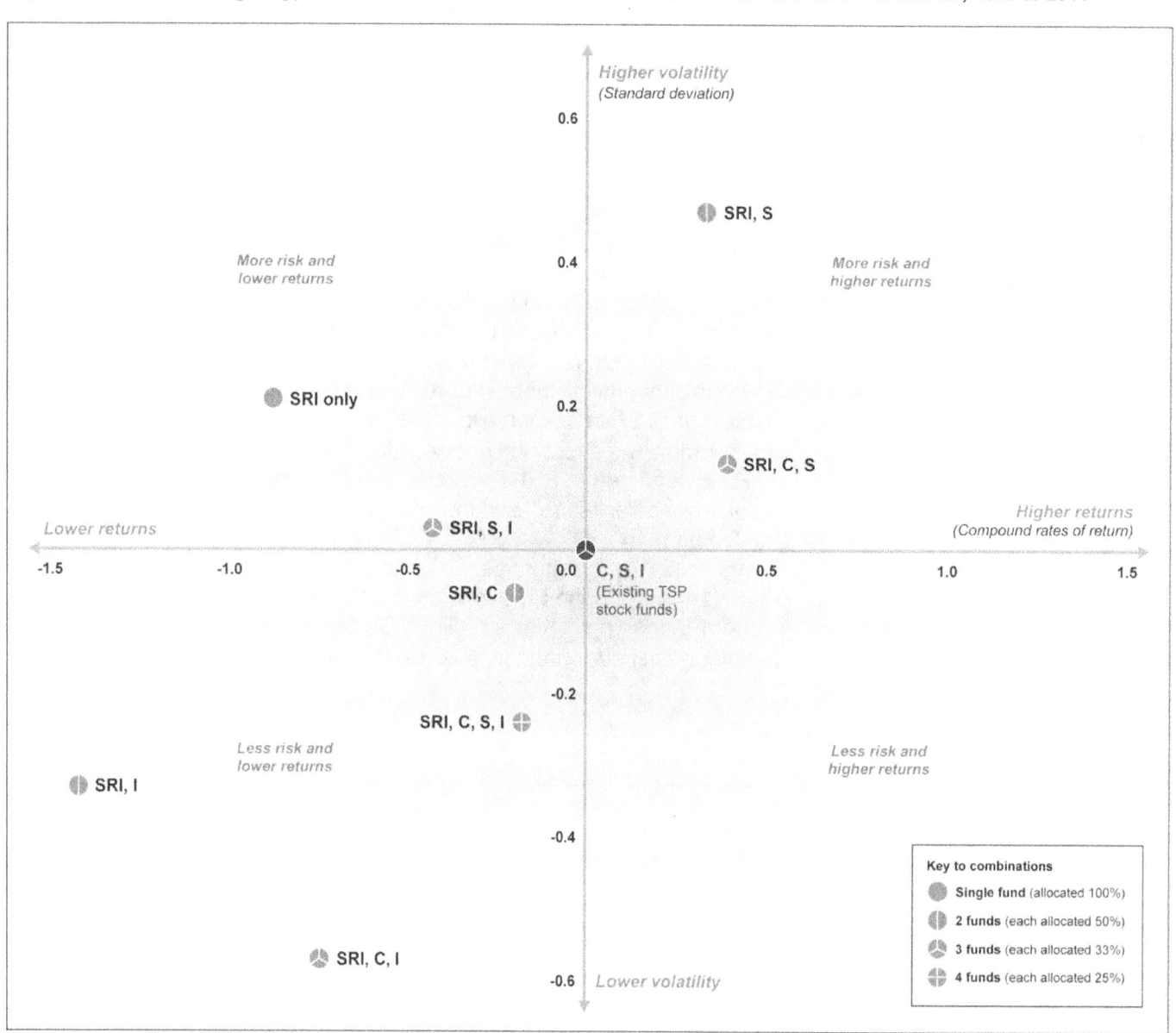

Source: GAO analysis of annual rates of total return based on monthly total return data from Morningstar, Inc.

Notes

1. We used a time-weighted basis for our analysis and rebalanced portfolios annually to maintain the evenly distributed allocations. A time-weighted basis gives equal weight to each unit of time; thus, the annual rate of return in 1992 gets just as much weight in the analysis as the annual rate of return in 2011. We used a time-weighted analysis in order to focus on investment performance itself, rather than on the particular economic consequences in the time period under study. For a TSP participant, the overall compound rate of return would be affected by interim cash flow into and out of the plan. For example, for a TSP participant who made regular contributions to the plan during the 1992 to 2011 period, the overall rate of return would be more influenced by particular performance in the later years, when more contributions are at stake, than in the earlier years.

2. In this figure, returns represent annualized compound return (i.e., geometric average annual return), while volatility represents standard deviation of annual return.

Overall, portfolio performance is directly tied to the individual fund performance, which varied by time period. A comparison of the underlying indices of these four funds shows that, while the SRI Fund had higher cumulative returns than the I Fund over the last 20 years, it had lower cumulative returns than all three of the TSP funds over the last 10 years. Figure 5 shows the funds' annual and cumulative returns and highlights their performance during market cycles.

Figure 5: Annual and Cumulative Returns of the Indices Underlying the C, S, I, and SRI Funds, 1992 to 2011

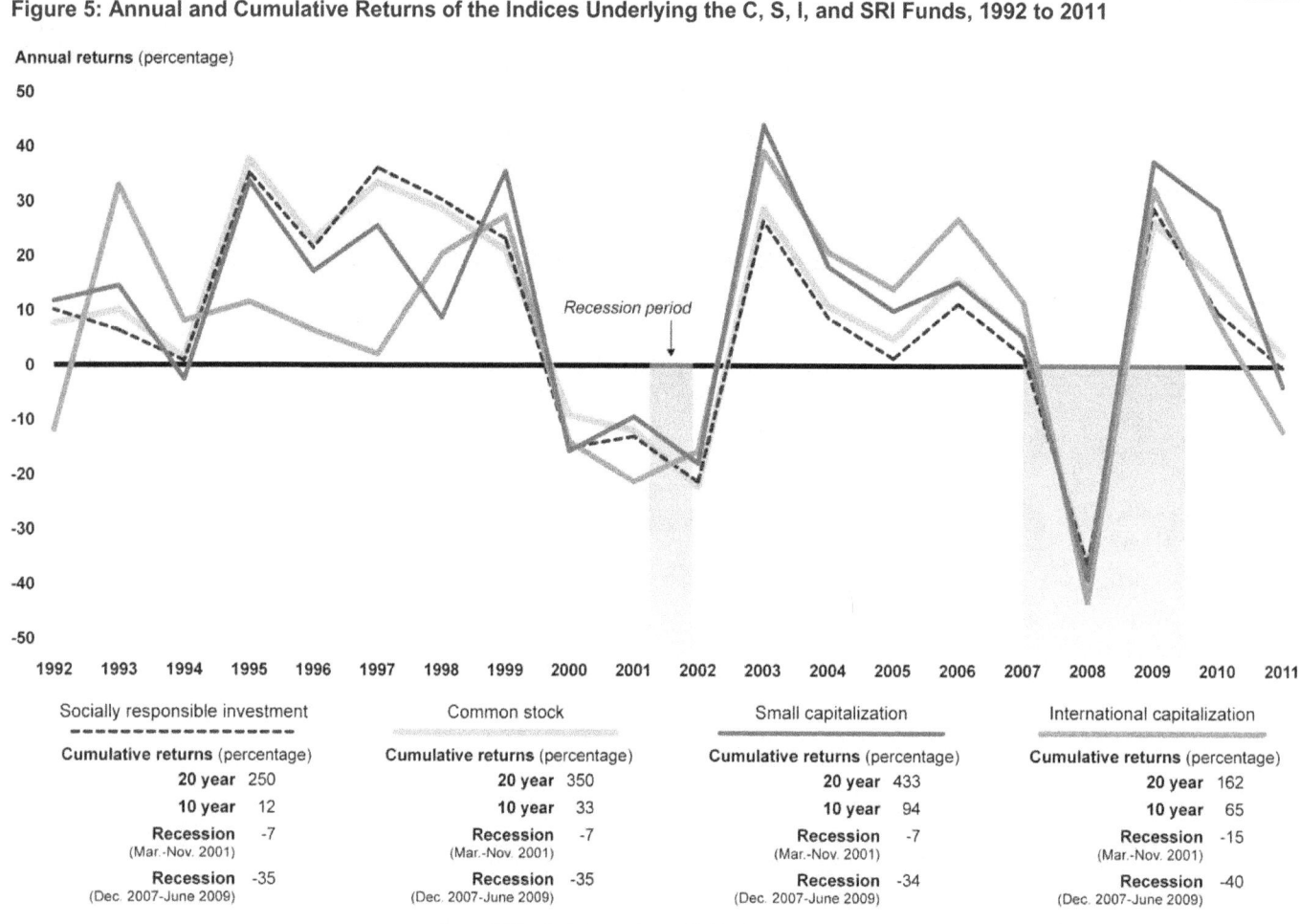

Source: GAO analysis of annual rates of total return based on monthly total return data from Morningstar, Inc.

The managers of the SRI index explained the difference in the index's performance over the last 20 years in comparison with the Standard & Poor's 500 Index (the C Fund index) was a result of having different sector weightings than the overall market to align with the fund's SRI strategy. For example, they told us that, in the late 1990s, the index was relatively overweighted in technology, consumer, and finance stocks and underweighted in energy and utilities, resulting in higher performance in the "dot com" boom of the late 1990s and lower performance in the 2001 recession. Moreover, the SRI index also excludes companies involved in the production of military weapons, which may have contributed to lower returns over the past decade while the country has been at war.

In addition to providing less return overall than the C Fund over the 20-year period, the inclusion of this SRI Fund would have resulted in overlap with the C Fund and not have provided a substantial opportunity for additional portfolio diversification.[27] By law, holdings in TSP stock funds may not overlap. Fifty-seven percent of the companies included in the SRI Fund index, which includes large, mid, and small capitalization stocks, overlap with companies included in the C Fund index.[28] In part, as a result of this overlap, the SRI Fund and the C Fund are highly correlated in their returns, and thus adding this SRI Fund would not provide a substantial opportunity for additional portfolio diversification. Portfolio diversification aims to reduce risk by investing in various financial instruments and markets so that market events will not affect all assets in the same way. Diversification opportunities exist if investments have independent price movement, and therefore, independent returns. The price movement between these two funds over the last 20 years was 1.94 percent independent, suggesting that the same external causes affected their returns to nearly the same degree.[29] By contrast, over the same time period, the independence in price movement between the S Fund and C Fund was 17.27 percent, and between the I Fund and C Fund was 42.19 percent.

---

[27]Investors may pursue SRI for reasons other than portfolio diversification, including directing their retirement savings to socially responsible companies.

[28]Other SRI indices may have had more or less overlap with the C Fund index.

[29]Price movements between two funds can be between 0 and 100 percent independent. The independence of price movements is measured by 100 percent independence of price movements less the common variance. The common variance is a statistical measure that measures independence of price movements, and is the square of the correlation coefficient. The correlation coefficient of the two funds was 0.99 over this time period. Correlation coefficient is a statistical measure that falls between -1.0 and +1.0. A coefficient of +1.0 means that the two indices move in the same direction at the same time in the same (relative) amounts.

SRI Mutual Fund Performance Varied by Asset Class, but Had Similar Costs to Non-SRI Mutual Funds

After Controlling for Fund Size and Strategy, SRI Bond Mutual Funds and SRI Stock Mutual Funds Outperformed Their Non-SRI Counterparts

Looking more broadly at SRI mutual funds, the most common form of SRI in the United States, we found that the comparative performance of SRI and non-SRI mutual funds over the last 15 years varied by asset class. While TSP participants cannot currently invest in mutual funds through TSP, the Board is authorized to offer a mutual fund window if it determines that it is in the best interests of participants. Specifically, our analysis of institutional-grade mutual funds[30] over the last 5, 10, and 15 years (dating back from December 2011) found that SRI bond mutual funds had better risk-adjusted performance than their non-SRI counterparts. In contrast, SRI stock funds and SRI balanced funds—which hold bonds and stocks—had worse risk-adjusted performance than their non-SRI counterparts over these time periods.[31] Because this analysis is strictly based on past performance, these results do not

---

[30]Morningstar identified three share classes of mutual funds—institutional, front-load and no-load—as the most common share classes used by institutional investors. We refer to these three share classes together as institutional grade mutual funds. We did not analyze other forms of SRI funds such as variable annuities and exchange traded funds. Hence, the results of our analysis are not generalizable to non-institutional grade mutual funds or to other forms of SRI. We included three asset classes of mutual funds in our analysis, stocks, bonds, and balanced. Stock funds invest in stocks, bond funds invest in bonds, and balanced funds invest in a combination of stocks and bonds. Looking at institutional grade share classes of mutual funds, we identified: (1) 21 SRI bond mutual funds, 118 SRI stock mutual funds, and 30 SRI balanced mutual funds, and (2) 2,403 non-SRI bond mutual funds, 3,579 non-SRI stock mutual funds, and 1,366 non-SRI balanced mutual funds active as of December 2011.

[31]In this section, risk-adjusted returns are measured by Sharpe and Sortino ratios. Sharpe ratio is calculated by using standard deviation and excess return to determine reward per unit of risk. The higher the Sharpe ratio is, the better the fund's historical risk-adjusted performance. The Sortino ratio differentiates harmful volatility from volatility in general by using a value for downside deviation. The Sortino ratio is the excess return over the risk-free rate divided by the downside semi-variance. For additional details on performance by asset class, see appendix III.

guarantee or imply that these asset classes would perform similarly in the future.

After controlling for fund size and investment strategies (other than SRI approaches), we found that the performance gap between the SRI and non-SRI mutual funds narrowed significantly for stock funds but not for balanced funds. Moreover, our regression estimates showed that SRI stock mutual funds performed better than their non-SRI stock counterparts in the 5- and 15-year timeframes, after controlling for differences in asset size, share class, and investment strategies.[32] (See appendix I for additional information on the regression analyses.)

SRI and Non-SRI Mutual Funds Had Similar Costs

In fiscal year 2010, the costs of SRI institutional grade mutual funds were similar to their non-SRI counterparts. It is important to note that our cost analysis included only the most recent year of data available (fiscal year 2010) for three share classes of institutional grade mutual funds, and it did not look at all SRI product types such as variable annuities or exchange traded funds, which may have had higher costs.[33] In addition, fiscal year 2010 cost data are not indicative of past or future costs. As shown in figure 7, there was considerable overlap in the costs associated with these funds, as measured by their annual net expense ratio—the actual percentage of assets deducted each fiscal year for fund expenses.[34]

---

[32]We ran regressions to control for fund size, share class, and investment strategy other than SRI approaches. The investment strategy control variables were whether a fund is actively managed or passively tracks an index, the broad investment category of a fund based on portfolio statistics and composition (e.g., natural resources, real estate, or financial), the more narrowly defined institutional investment category of a fund based on portfolio statistics and composition (e.g., materials, domestic energy, or technology), and the market capitalization and type of stock (value, blend, and growth).

[33]We ran cost regressions to control for fund size, share class, and investment strategy other than SRI approaches.

[34]According to Morningstar, the annual net expense ratio reflects the actual fees charged during a particular fiscal year. The expense ratio is expressed as the percentage of assets deducted each fiscal year for fund expenses.

Figure 6: Comparison of Annual Net Expense Ratios of SRI and Non-SRI Mutual Funds

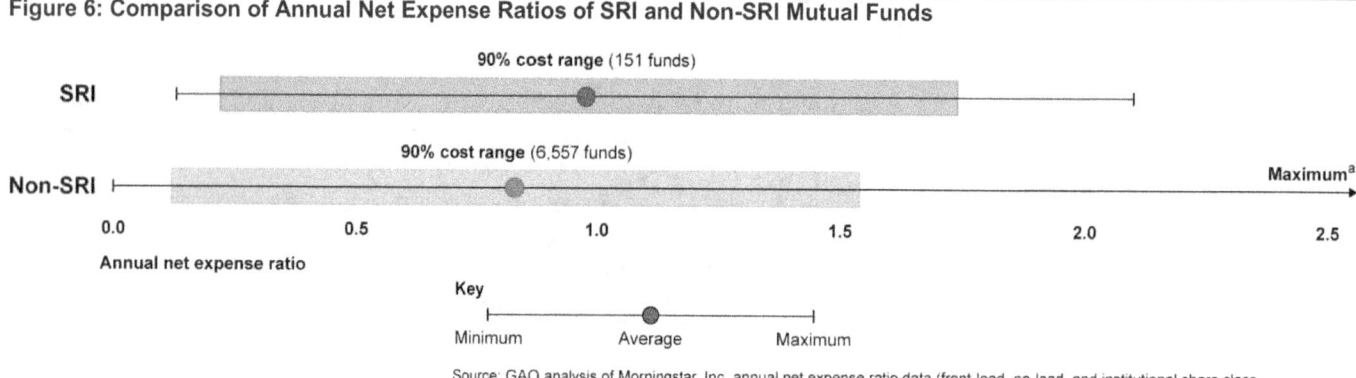

Source: GAO analysis of Morningstar, Inc. annual net expense ratio data (front-load, no-load, and institutional share class mutual funds only).

[a]The non-SRI maximum annual net expense ratio was 7.93 percent

While non-SRI mutual funds had a broader range of costs than SRI mutual funds, the vast majority of SRI and non-SRI funds reported expense ratios from 0.12 to 1.81 percent. On average, the reported expense ratios for SRI mutual funds were 0.2 percentage points higher than non-SRI mutual funds.[35] When asset size and investment strategy were taken into account, SRI mutual fund cost ratios were estimated to be only 0.06 percentage points higher than non-SRI mutual fund cost ratios.[36] For additional details on our regression analysis on cost ratios, see appendix I.

Concluding Observations

Adoption of an SRI index fund would present challenges for TSP. Currently, the law limits the types of funds that TSP can offer, prohibits overlap among existing funds, and charges TSP to keep its costs low. First, TSP would have difficulty finding an SRI index fund that did not overlap with the existing TSP funds, limiting opportunities for additional portfolio diversification. However, officials at other DC plans, which do not face the same restrictions as TSP, said that a certain amount of overlap with SRI and other investment options was acceptable and the purpose of SRI was to provide an alternative investment choice. Second, TSP would have difficulty selecting SRI screening criteria that all participants and the

---

[35]In fiscal year 2010, SRI mutual funds had an average net-expense ratio of 1.08 percent and non-SRI mutual had an average net-expense ratio of 0.88 percent.

[36]We ran cost regressions to control for fund size, share class, and investment strategy other than SRI approaches.

Congress would find acceptable. While challenging, a number of plans have a long history of SRI in their plans. Finally, under TSP's current structure, the costs of adding a new fund would be distributed among all participants regardless of whether they participated in that fund. We note that the Board has the authority to open a mutual fund window for participants to invest in mutual funds managed outside TSP. If the Board decides to act on this authority and allow the mutual fund window, participants seeking other forms of investment, including SRI, could invest in mutual funds and would bear the costs associated with this investment.

Agency Comments

We provided a copy of this draft report to the Federal Retirement Thrift Investment Board, the Department of Labor, and the Department of the Treasury for review and comment. None of the agencies provided formal comments. The Department of Labor provided technical comments, which we incorporated in the report, as appropriate.

As agreed with your office, unless you publicly announce its contents earlier, we plan no further distribution of this report until 30 days from its issue date. At that time, we will send copies of this report to relevant congressional committees and other interested parties. In addition, this report will be available at no charge on GAO's website at http://www.gao.gov.

If you or your staff have any questions about this report, please contact me at (202) 512-7215 or jeszeckc@gao.gov. Contact points for our Offices of Congressional Relations and Public Affairs may be found on the last page of this report. GAO staff making key contributions to this report is listed in appendix IV.

Sincerely yours,

Charles A. Jeszeck
Director
Education, Workforce,
   and Income Security Issues

Appendix I: Objectives, Scope, and Methodology

To determine the challenges associated with socially responsible investment (SRI), we reviewed relevant federal laws, regulations, and literature. For example, we reviewed the Federal Employees' Retirement System Act of 1986, the Federal Retirement Reform Act of 2009, and the 2006 United Nations' *Principles for Responsible Investment*. We also interviewed officials from the Thrift Savings Plan (TSP), the Employee Thrift Advisory Council, investment management and consultant firms, and 15 selected public pension plans. Our nonrepresentative sample of pension plans included 9 domestic defined contribution (DC) and defined benefit (DB) plans that incorporated SRI, and 6 plans that considered but did not adopt an SRI component. To identify our sample, we contacted plans that were signatories of the United Nations' *Principles for Responsible Investment* and employed a snowball sampling technique based on recommendations of interviewees. We analyzed interview responses of pension plan officials and other SRI experts on the challenges and benefits associated with SRI, and how these experiences might affect TSP.

To determine how the addition of an SRI index fund to a TSP stock portfolio would have affected past TSP stock portfolio performance, we identified the best performing U.S.-based SRI index and assessed its potential impact on the TSP stock portfolio based on historical performance data of the three TSP stock fund underlying indices.[1] To identify the best performing U.S.-based SRI stock index (SRI Fund) we (1) identified all U.S.-based SRI stock indices with at least a 10-year history, and (2) selected the index with the best 10-year Sharpe ratio (dating back from December 2011).[2] To determine how the SRI Fund would have affected TSP stock portfolio performance from 1992 to 2011, we analyzed monthly total return data for the SRI Fund and the underlying indices of the three TSP stock funds provided by Morningstar, Inc.—a leading independent financial market research firm. We used these data to analyze changes in annual returns and volatility, in a manner similar to past analysis conducted by TSP when considering whether to add funds

---

[1]The Common Stock Index Investment Fund (C Fund) is indexed to the Standard & Poor's 500 Index. The Small Capitalization Stock Index Investment Fund (S Fund) is indexed to the Dow Jones U.S. Completion Total Stock Market Index. The International Stock Index Investment Fund (I Fund) is indexed to the Morgan Stanley Capital International Europe, Australasia, and Far East Index.

[2]We selected the best performing SRI stock index from the five U.S.-based SRI stock indices with at least a 10-year history that were active as of December 2011. Sharpe ratio is calculated by using standard deviation and excess return to determine reward per unit of risk. As such, the higher the Sharpe ratio, the better the fund's historical risk-adjusted performance.

to the TSP portfolio. An important element of any performance statistic is the
unit of time measurement. Our analysis measures returns on an annual
basis, and measures risk based on the variation in year-to-year returns.
Using a different unit of time, such as a month or even a multi-year period,
could give a different picture of the risk/reward tradeoff. We calculated the
compound rates of return and standard deviation[3] based on annual rates of
return from 1992 to 2011 for an annually rebalanced, evenly distributed
portfolio of the three existing TSP stock fund indices (a distribution of 33
percent, 33 percent, and 33 percent). We then calculated the change in
compound rates of return and standard deviation of annual returns for the
following evenly distributed portfolios:

- a four-way combination (25 percent, 25 percent, 25 percent, and 25
  percent) of the SRI Fund and the three TSP stock funds indices,

- all of the three-way combinations (33 percent, 33 percent, and 33
  percent) of the SRI Fund with two of the TSP stock fund indices,

- all two-way combinations (50 percent and 50 percent) of the SRI Fund
  with one of the TSP stock fund indices, and

- the SRI Fund alone (100 percent).

Another decision in any performance assessment is whether to do the
analysis on a time-weighted or a dollar-weighted basis. A time-weighted
basis gives equal weight to each unit of time; thus, the annual rate of
return in 1992 gets just as much weight in the analysis as the annual rate
of return in 2011. A dollar-weighted basis gives greater weight to the
periods when more money is at stake. For example, for a TSP participant
who made regular contributions to the plan during the 1992 to 2011
period, the overall rate of return would be more influenced by particular
performance in the later years, when more contributions are at stake,
than in the earlier years. We used a time-weighted basis for our analysis,
in order to focus on investment performance itself, rather than on the
particular economic consequences in the time period under study.

---

[3]Specifically, we calculated annualized compound return (i.e., geometric average annual
return) and standard deviation of annual return. Standard deviation is a statistical measure
of the range of a fund's performance. When a fund has a high standard deviation, its
range of performance has been very wide, indicating that there is a greater potential for
volatility.

To further assess the performance of the SRI Fund, we compared annual rates of return and compound cumulative rates of return for the three TSP stock fund indices over various time periods. Specifically, we reviewed performance over the 20-year period (1992 to 2011), the 10-year period (2002 to 2011), and periods of market weakness. Because this analysis is strictly based on past performance, this result does not guarantee or imply that the addition of an SRI index would have the same effect on future TSP stock fund portfolio performance. In addition, we analyzed the overlap of holdings of the SRI Fund and the C Fund as of April 2012. To analyze the diversification potential of the SRI Fund for the TSP stock portfolio, we analyzed the correlation coefficient, common variance, and independence of price movement between the SRI Fund and the C Fund over the last 20 years.[4]

To determine how the performance and cost of SRI mutual funds compare with those of non-SRI mutual funds, we compared performance over the past 15 years (1997 to 2011)— the longest time period for which data were available—and costs as of fiscal year 2010 provided by Morningstar. To identify the universe of SRI mutual funds, we included mutual funds from Morningstar considered to be SRI mutual funds based on ethical screen employed and data on SRI mutual funds maintained by US SIF.[5] To analyze performance and cost of SRI and non-SRI mutual funds active as of December 2011, we focused our analysis exclusively on three institutional grade share classes—institutional, front-load and no-load—of U.S. domiciled open-end mutual funds, which experts identified as the most common form of SRI funds. We did not examine other forms of SRI, such as exchange traded funds, hedge funds, or variable annuities. Because this analysis is strictly based on past performance, these results do not guarantee or imply that these asset classes would perform similarly in the future. Performance statistics include measures of risk-adjusted returns over 5-, 10-, and 15-year time periods dating back from December 2011.

---

[4]Correlation coefficient is a statistical measure that falls between -1.0 and +1.0. A coefficient of +1.0 means that the two indices move in the same direction at the same time in the same (relative) amounts. The independence of price movements is measured by 100 percent independence of price movements less the common variance. The common variance is a statistical measure that measures independence of price movements, and is the square of the correlation coefficient.

[5]US SIF was formerly the Social Investment Forum (SIF). US SIF is a U.S. membership association for professionals, firms, institutions and organizations engaged in sustainable and responsible investing.

Some mutual funds had more recent inception dates, thus limiting the number of funds in longer-term performance comparisons. Risk-adjusted return statistics include the Sharpe and Sortino ratios. Cost measures include fiscal year 2010 annual report net-expense ratios.[6]

To investigate why SRI and non-SRI mutual funds differed in performance, we ran regressions with and without controls for fund size, share class, and investment strategy not inherently related to SRI. We used the risk-adjusted performance measures, Sharpe and Sortino ratios, as the dependent variables. Table 2 summarizes the results of 24 regressions for U.S. stock funds. The numbers in the columns labeled "Outcome Variable 1" and "Outcome Variable 2" are coefficient estimates on a flag indicating that a fund was non-SRI.[7]

Table 2: Regression Coefficients on Non-SRI Indicator: U.S. Stock Funds, Institutional, Front-load, and No-load Share Classes

Time frame and control variables	Outcome variable 1, Sharpe ratio	Outcome variable 2, Sortino ratio	Average percentage change in non-SRI coefficient with controls
5-year, without control variables	0.014	0.017	
with fund size	0.001	-0.001	-100%
with strategy categories	0.009	0.010	-37
with all controls	-0.004	-0.008	-139
10-year, without control variables	0.077	0.110	
with fund size	0.054	0.077	-30
with strategy categories	0.044	0.061	-44
with all controls	0.02	0.027	-75
15-year, without control variables	0.026	0.037	

---

[6]Annual report expense ratios reflect the actual fees charged during a particular fiscal year. The expense ratio expresses the percentage of assets deducted each fiscal year for fund expenses.

[7]We do not report standard errors of estimates here because our results are based on the universe of mutual funds that fit our criteria, rather than a sample. Thus standard errors are not applicable.

Time frame and control variables	Outcome variable 1, Sharpe ratio	Outcome variable 2, Sortino ratio	Average percentage change in non-SRI coefficient with controls
with fund size	0.002	0.002	-95
with strategy categories	0.009	0.011	-68
with all controls	-0.015	-0.024	-161
Average change in coefficient across all time periods with inclusion of fund size categories			-75
Average change in coefficient across all time periods with inclusion of fund strategy control variables			-50
Average change in coefficient across all time periods with inclusion of full set of controls			-125

Source: GAO analysis of data received from Morningstar, Inc.

As shown above, the Sharpe ratio served as the outcome variable for the first set of regressions (second column of the table). The Sortino ratio served as the outcome variable for the second set of regressions (third column of the table). The last column shows the average impact on the non-SRI flag coefficient of inclusion of the control variables for the row. For each outcome variable, inclusion of the control variables generally reduced the estimated performance premium of non-SRI funds versus SRI funds. The fund size and strategy variable sets both had substantial impacts on the estimated difference in SRI and non-SRI fund performance.

The rows of the table show regression results for the 5-, 10-, and 15-year time frames. The rows indicating no control variables included only the non-SRI flag. The rows indicating "with fund size" included fund size, along with the SRI variable as explanatory variables.[8] The row indicating "with strategy categories" include controls for whether a fund is actively managed or passively tracks an index, the broad investment category of a fund based on portfolio statistics and composition (e.g., natural resources, real estate, or financial), the more narrowly defined institutional investment category of a fund based on portfolio statistics and

---

[8]The size intervals were determined using an SPSS Decision Tree algorithm. The algorithm found six size categories which differed significantly from each other in the ratio of SRI to non-SRI funds. Breaking fund size into categories allowed including funds without fund size data in the analysis, because the missing data were grouped into a category.

composition (e.g., materials, domestic energy, technology, or utilities), and the market capitalization and type of stock (value, blend, and growth). The row indicating "with all controls" provides results for regressions with share class as an explanatory variable in addition to the fund size and strategy variables.[9]

Table 3 shows results from 24 regressions for balanced funds. The methodology for these regressions was the same as that used for the regressions in table 2. Accounting for covariates did not have a consistent impact on the estimated difference in performance between SRI and non-SRI funds for these funds, with the addition of control variables to the regressions sometimes increasing the estimated difference in performance and sometimes decreasing it.

Table 3: Regression Coefficients on Non-SRI Indicator: U.S. Balanced Funds, Institutional, Front-load, and No-load Share Classes

Time frame and control variables	Outcome variable 1 Sharpe ratio	Outcome variable 2 Sortino ratio	Average percentage change in non-SRI coefficient with controls
5-year, without control variables	0.057	0.082	
with fund size	0.040	0.060	-28%
with strategy categories	0.078	0.112	37
with all controls	0.063	0.09	10
10-year, without control variables	0.164	0.241	
with fund size	0.130	0.191	-21
with strategy categories	0.148	0.217	-1
with all controls	0.125	0.185	-23
15-year, without control variables	0.111	0.166	
with fund size	0.056	0.083	-50
with strategy categories	0.094	0.139	-16
with all controls	0.063	0.093	-43
Average change in coefficient across all time periods with inclusion of fund size categories			-33

[9]We did not include standard deviation as an explanatory variable in the regressions because volatility is accounted for in the risk-adjusted performance measures.

Time frame and control variables	Outcome variable 1 Sharpe ratio	Outcome variable 2 Sortino ratio	Average percentage change in non-SRI coefficient with controls
Average change in coefficient across all time periods with inclusion of fund strategy control variables			4
Average change in coefficient across all time periods with inclusion of full set of controls			-19

Source: GAO analysis of data received from Morningstar, Inc.

Table 4 shows results for 24 regressions for bond funds. The methodology for these regressions was the same as that used for the regressions in table 2 except that one field (equity style box) was not included as an explanatory variable because it was not populated for 90 percent of these funds. Accounting for covariates generally decreased the estimated difference in performance between the SRI and non-SRI funds.

Table 4: Regression Coefficients on Non-SRI Indicator: U.S. Bond Funds, Institutional, Front-load, and No-load Share Classes

Time frame and control variables	Outcome variable 1 Sharpe ratio	Outcome variable 2 Sortino ratio	Average percentage change in non-SRI coefficient with controls
5-year, without control variables	-0.264	-0.452	
with fund size	-0.277	-0.486	-6%
with strategy categories	-0.028	0.055	101
with all controls	-0.028	0.037	99
10-year, without control variables	-0.154	-0.222	
with fund size	-0.159	-0.235	-5
with strategy categories	-0.006	0.047	109
with all controls	-0.005	0.045	109
15-year, without control variables	-0.252	-0.380	
with fund size	-0.250	-0.375	1
with strategy categories	-0.071	-0.085	75
with all controls	-0.065	-0.072	78
Average change in coefficient across all time periods with inclusion of fund size variables			-3

Time frame and control variables	Outcome variable 1 Sharpe ratio	Outcome variable 2 Sortino ratio	Average percentage change in non-SRI coefficient with controls
Average change in coefficient across all time periods with inclusion of fund strategy control variables			95
Average change in coefficient across all time periods with inclusion of full set of controls			95

Source: GAO analysis of data received from Morningstar, Inc.

To investigate disparities between SRI and non-SRI mutual fund costs, we ran regressions that controlled for fund size, share class, and investment strategy. The coefficient for a flag indicating SRI status is reported for four regressions in table 5. The regression reported in the third column used fund size categories along with the SRI variable as explanatory variables. The strategy variables used in the regressions reported in the fourth and fifth columns were the same as those used for the performance regressions reported above. Once the fund size and investment strategy variables are taken into account, the estimated difference in cost between SRI and non-SRI funds falls to 0.06 percent.

Table 5: Coefficient on SRI Indicator in Regression with Annual Report Net Expense Ratio as Dependent Variable With and Without Control Variables

		Control variables		
	No control variables	Fund size categories	Strategy variables	Strategy share class, and fund size categories
Estimated percentage point difference in cost between SRI and non-SRI mutual funds	0.20	0.15	0.12	0.06

Source: GAO analysis of mutual fund annual report net-expense ratio data received from Morningstar Inc.

We assessed the reliability of the quantitative data used in this engagement provided by Morningstar by reviewing related documentation, interviewing knowledgeable officials, reviewing related internal controls, comparing to published data, and tracing a selection of data to source documentation. Based on this evaluation, we determined these data were reliable for the purposes of this report. We supplemented our quantitative analysis with qualitative data obtained from our interviews.

Appendix II: Variation of Annual Compound Rates of Return and Standard Deviation among Evenly Distributed Allocations of the Best Performing SRI Stock Index and Existing TSP Stock Index Funds, 1992 through 2011

Allocations	Change in compound rate of return from baseline (percentage per year)	Change in standard deviation from baseline (percentage overall)
Existing TSP Funds (C, S, I) (baseline)	0.00	0.00
SRI ,C, S, I	-0.18	-0.24
SRI, C, I	-0.75	-0.57
SRI, C, S	0.39	0.12
SRI, S, I	-0.43	0.03
SRI, C	-0.20	-0.06
SRI, S	0.33	0.47
SRI, I	-1.42	-0.33
SRI Fund only	-0.88	0.21
C Fund only	0.46	-0.24
S Fund only	1.38	1.79
I Fund only	-2.41	2.00

Source: GAO analysis of annual rates of total return based on monthly total return data from Morningstar, Inc.

Appendix III: Additional Information on the Performance of SRI and Non-SRI Mutual Funds by Asset Class

Our analysis of institutional-grade mutual funds over the last 5, 10, and 15 years (dating back from December 2011) showed that SRI bond mutual funds had better risk-adjusted performance than their non-SRI counterparts, while SRI stock and SRI balanced funds did not.[1] Specifically, we reviewed measures of risk-adjusted performance including the Sharpe and Sortino ratios. Morningstar Inc. defines these ratios as follows:

- *Sharpe ratio.* This statistic is a reward to variability ratio, which offers a means of locating an optimal risky portfolio. The equation is:

$$s = \frac{r_A - r_F}{\sigma}$$

rA= expected return on the series or portfolio

σ= the standard deviation

rF= the risk-free rate

And where standard deviation is:

$$\sigma_y = \sqrt{\frac{1}{n-1} \sum_{t=1}^{n} r_t - \ddot{r}^2}$$

---

[1]Morningstar identified three share classes of mutual funds—institutional, front-load and no-load—as the most common share classes used by institutional investors. We refer to these three share classes together as institutional grade mutual funds. We did not analyze other forms of SRI funds such as variable annuities and exchange traded funds. Hence, the results of our analysis are not generalizable to non-institutional grade mutual funds or to other forms of SRI. We included three asset classes of mutual funds in our analysis, stocks, bonds, and balanced. Stock funds invest in stocks, bond funds invest in bonds, and balanced funds invest in a combination of stocks and bonds. After controlling for fund size and investment strategies (other than SRI approaches), we found that the gap between the performance of SRI and non-SRI mutual funds narrowed significantly for stock funds but not for balanced funds.

**Appendix III: Additional Information on the
Performance of SRI and Non-SRI Mutual Funds
by Asset Class**

Where:

σ= the Greek letter commonly used to denote standard deviation

rt= expected return on the series or portfolio

$\bar{r}$= the arithmetic mean of the return series r

n= the number of periods

- *Sortino ratio.* The Sortino ratio is a risk adjusted return ratio that considers excess return over a designated target return and the risk of not achieving that target return. Excess return is defined as the series' return less the target return; risk is considered to be the semi-standard deviation below the target return. The Sortino ratio therefore tells you how well you are being compensated by a series for each unit of shortfall risk you are incurring.

  The formula for the Sortino ratio:

  Where:

  T= target return

  SD= the target semi-standard deviation of the return series in question over the period in question. This is the square root of the target semi-variance, with T as the target return

  $\overline{R_p}$ the arithmetic average return of the return series in question over the period in question

Appendix III: Additional Information on the
Performance of SRI and Non-SRI Mutual Funds
by Asset Class

The following tables provide additional information on risk-adjusted performance of SRI and non-SRI mutual funds by asset class.

Bond Mutual Funds

Table 6: Sharpe Ratio SRI and Non-SRI Bond Mutual Funds

Type of fund	Measure	Annualized time period		
		5 year	10 year	15 year
SRI				
	Mean	1.02	0.82	0.77
	Median	1.00	0.87	0.75
	Maximum	1.53	1.20	0.84
	Minimum	0.27	0.38	0.73
	Number	18	17	4
Non-SRI				
	Mean	0.76	0.66	0.52
	Median	0.68	0.64	0.48
	Maximum	2.82	2.05	1.84
	Minimum	-2.98	-2.09	-2.71
	Number	2,103	1,799	1,449

Source: GAO analysis of mutual fund performance data received from Morningstar, Inc.

Table 7: Sortino Ratio SRI and Non-SRI Bond Mutual Funds

Type of fund	Measure	Annualized time period		
		5 year	10 year	15 year
SRI				
	Mean	1.80	1.27	1.19
	Median	1.69	1.32	1.19
	Maximum	3.01	2.15	1.28
	Minimum	0.36	0.51	1.09
	Number	18	17	4
Non-SRI				
	Mean	1.35	1.05	0.81
	Median	1.04	0.96	0.71
	Maximum	14.80	3.96	3.69
	Minimum	-2.48	-2.60	-2.76
	Number	2,103	1,799	1,449

Source: GAO analysis of mutual fund performance data received from Morningstar, Inc.

Appendix III: Additional Information on the
Performance of SRI and Non-SRI Mutual Funds
by Asset Class

Stock Mutual Funds

Table 8: Sharpe Ratio SRI and Non-SRI Stock Mutual Funds

Type of fund	Measure	Annualized time period		
		5 year	10 year	15 year
SRI				
	Mean	0.05	0.14	0.24
	Median	0.06	0.12	0.23
	Maximum	0.33	0.52	0.47
	Minimum	-0.49	-0.05	-0.01
	Number	86	68	37
Non-SRI				
	Mean	0.07	0.22	0.27
	Median	0.06	0.20	0.26
	Maximum	0.73	0.68	0.72
	Minimum	-0.94	-0.38	-0.13
	Number	3,165	2,466	1,431

Source: GAO analysis of mutual fund performance data received from Morningstar, Inc.

Table 9: Sortino Ratio SRI and Non-SRI Stock Mutual Funds

Type of fund	Measure	Annualized time period		
		5 year	10 year	15 year
SRI				
	Mean	0.08	0.20	0.35
	Median	0.09	0.17	0.33
	Maximum	0.50	0.78	0.69
	Minimum	-0.57	-0.06	-0.01
	Number	86	68	37
Non-SRI				
	Mean	0.10	0.31	0.39
	Median	0.09	0.28	0.37
	Maximum	1.29	1.04	1.12
	Minimum	-1.02	-0.45	-0.16
	Number	3,165	2,466	1,431

Source: GAO analysis of mutual fund performance data received from Morningstar, Inc.

**Appendix III: Additional Information on the
Performance of SRI and Non-SRI Mutual Funds
by Asset Class**

Balanced Mutual Funds

Table 10: Sharpe Ratio SRI and Non-SRI Balanced Mutual Funds

Type of fund	Measure	Annualized time period		
		5 year	10 year	15 year
SRI				
	Mean	0.05	0.13	0.21
	Median	0.02	0.15	0.20
	Maximum	0.38	0.23	0.36
	Minimum	-0.15	-0.16	-0.02
	Number	20	13	8
Non-SRI				
	Mean	0.11	0.29	0.32
	Median	0.09	0.27	0.30
	Maximum	0.89	0.95	0.78
	Minimum	-1.20	-1.18	-0.93
	Number	897	454	318

Source: GAO analysis of mutual fund performance data received from Morningstar, Inc.

Table 11: Sortino Ratio SRI and Non-SRI Balanced Mutual Funds

Type of fund	Measure	Annualized time period		
		5 year	10 year	15 year
SRI				
	Mean	0.07	0.18	0.29
	Median	0.02	0.20	0.28
	Maximum	0.57	0.31	0.51
	Minimum	-0.19	-0.20	-0.03
	Number	20	13	8
Non-SRI				
	Mean	0.16	0.42	0.45
	Median	0.12	0.38	0.42
	Maximum	1.57	1.64	1.32
	Minimum	-1.26	-1.16	-1.00
	Number	897	454	318

Source: GAO analysis of mutual fund performance data received from Morningstar, Inc.

Appendix IV: GAO Contact and Staff Acknowledgment

GAO Contact	Charles A. Jeszeck, (202) 512-7215 or jeszeckc@gao.gov
Staff Acknowledgment	In addition to the individual named above, Kimberley Granger, Assistant Director; Jonathan S. McMurray, Analyst-in-Charge; James Bennett; and Sarah Kaczmarek made significant contributions to this report. Kenneth Stockbridge, Roger Thomas, and Jack Wang also made key contributions.

GAO's Mission	The Government Accountability Office, the audit, evaluation, and investigative arm of Congress, exists to support Congress in meeting its constitutional responsibilities and to help improve the performance and accountability of the federal government for the American people. GAO examines the use of public funds; evaluates federal programs and policies; and provides analyses, recommendations, and other assistance to help Congress make informed oversight, policy, and funding decisions. GAO's commitment to good government is reflected in its core values of accountability, integrity, and reliability.
Obtaining Copies of GAO Reports and Testimony	The fastest and easiest way to obtain copies of GAO documents at no cost is through GAO's website (www.gao.gov). Each weekday afternoon, GAO posts on its website newly released reports, testimony, and correspondence. To have GAO e-mail you a list of newly posted products, go to www.gao.gov and select "E-mail Updates."
Order by Phone	The price of each GAO publication reflects GAO's actual cost of production and distribution and depends on the number of pages in the publication and whether the publication is printed in color or black and white. Pricing and ordering information is posted on GAO's website, http://www.gao.gov/ordering.htm. Place orders by calling (202) 512-6000, toll free (866) 801-7077, or TDD (202) 512-2537. Orders may be paid for using American Express, Discover Card, MasterCard, Visa, check, or money order. Call for additional information.
Connect with GAO	Connect with GAO on Facebook, Flickr, Twitter, and YouTube. Subscribe to our RSS Feeds or E-mail Updates. Listen to our Podcasts. Visit GAO on the web at www.gao.gov.
To Report Fraud, Waste, and Abuse in Federal Programs	Contact: Website: www.gao.gov/fraudnet/fraudnet.htm E-mail: fraudnet@gao.gov Automated answering system: (800) 424-5454 or (202) 512-7470
Congressional Relations	Katherine Siggerud, Managing Director, siggerudk@gao.gov, (202) 512-4400, U.S. Government Accountability Office, 441 G Street NW, Room 7125, Washington, DC 20548
Public Affairs	Chuck Young, Managing Director, youngc1@gao.gov, (202) 512-4800 U.S. Government Accountability Office, 441 G Street NW, Room 7149 Washington, DC 20548

Please Print on Recycled Paper.